annual publication
useful information
↓

BLOOD ALMANAC

the life in farming

ANHINGA PRESS, 2006
TALLAHASSEE, FLORIDA

BLOOD ALMANAC

SANDY LONGHORN

2005 ANHINGA PRIZE FOR POETRY

Selected by Reginald Shepherd

ANHINGA PRESS, 2006
TALLAHASSEE, FLORIDA

Author Photograph: © George Byron Griffiths
Cover Photograph: © George Byron Griffiths,
                 from the "Harmony of the Gods" series
Cover design, book design, and production: C. L. Knight
Typesetting: Jill Ihasz
Type Styles: titles set in Tiepolo and text set in Minion

Library of Congress Cataloging-in-Publication Data
Blood Almanac by Sandy Longhorn – First Edition
ISBN – ISBN: 0-938078-91-7 (978-0-938078-91-3)

Library of Congress Cataloging Card Number – 2006924925

This publication is sponsored in part by a grant
from the Florida Department of State,
Division of Cultural Affairs, and the Florida Arts Council.

Anhinga Press Inc. is a nonprofit corporation dedicated wholly to the
publication and appreciation of fine poetry and other literary genres.

For personal orders, catalogs and information write to:
Anhinga Press
P.O. Box 10595
Tallahassee, Florida 32302
Web site: www.anhinga.org
E-mail: info@anhinga.org

Published in the United States
by Anhinga Press
Tallahassee, Florida
First Edition, 2006

*To my mother and father
and
for my beloved ~ CHW*

CONTENTS

LISTENING IN THE DARK

POSTSCRIPT

ACKNOWLEDGMENTS

Grateful acknowledgment is made to the editors and readers
of the following journals in which poems in this collection
have appeared or are forthcoming, sometimes in slightly
different form:

88: A Journal of Contemporary American Poetry: "Reckoning the
       Fragments," "Another Memory Fragment"
Arkansas Literary Forum: "April," "August," "Duty"
Arts & Letters: "Lover, Say *Prairie*"
Black Warrior Review: "February," "From the Outpost"
Boulevard: "December," "May"
CALYX: "Light," "Psalm for the Color Red"
Cincinnati Review: "Notes from the Cabin on Shiloh Mountain"
Crab Orchard Review: "Recitation During the Storm"
The Cream City Review: "Born Without," "June"
Fugue: "In Her Mother's Country"
Gulf Coast: "The Empty Set, Recurring"
Gulf Stream: "1976"
Hotel Amerika: "On the Great Plains' Eastern Edge"
Mangrove: "Sixty Miles to Peculiar"
Meridian: "Heliopause"
Midwest Quarterly: "Fence Line to Hill Rise"
RATTLE: "November"
River Styx: "March"
Smartish Pace: "Midnight Crossing Oklahoma,"
       "The Bridge at Burlington"
South Dakota Review: "Facing Home"
Sou'wester: "Etude"
Sycamore Review: "Labor Day on the Bremer Blacktop," "Inheritance"
Westview: "Black Dirt Girls," "Green Mountain Falls," "Roofing the
      Barn," "September"

A debt of gratitude is due to the following people for their commitment to this book and their support of my writing.

A heartfelt thanks to Tara Bray and Davis McCombs for reading and rereading — a part of this book belongs to them. Thanks to the rest of my teachers at the University of Arkansas as well — Miller Williams, Michael Heffernan, Jim Whitehead, and all the faculty, staff and students I met along the way. There are also those who offered emotional support — Gary and Sharon Longhorn, Mara Faulkner, Kirsten Day, Heather Quinney, Emöke Pulay, Anne Greenwood, James Katowich, Sean Chapman, Elizabeth Bryer, Allison Wolcott, Karen Helfrich, Marta Ferguson, Chris and Sue Lowell, Leslie Balvanz, and Janel Vandemore — my family, my friends, I thank you.

I will always be grateful to Reginald Shepherd for selecting this book and to Rick Campbell, Lynne Knight, and everyone at Anhinga for their support.

Above and beyond the rest — Chuck West.

BLOOD ALMANAC

BIRTHLIGHT

BLACK DIRT GIRLS

Nights we sat on the porch steps and peered out
into the moss-colored twilight. The tall grasses,
bent by heads bursting with grain, were lit
with hosts of lightning bugs tilting like drunks.
We kept our voices low, masked by the electric hum
of mosquito swarms and the staccato slap
of palms on skin where bites festered into hills.
In the window behind us a fan sliced the air's
invisible body and chopped at the dense silence —
he in the den, she leaning over the kitchen sink.
Two miles across the cornfields, truck traffic rattled
over Highway 63, the now-and-then screech
of brakes bringing our eyes up as if we could see
that far into the darkness or the future.

1976

Summer of the Bicentennial — shiny new quarters,
(diesel fumes and Swisher Sweets, Daddy's hand

on the tall gearshift of his snub-nosed Freightliner,
weeks on the road with nothing but the radio,

his coming home a ritual of air horn and hissing brakes.
One weekend he taught us the ways of the river,

how to force up the dead with the cast of a grappling hook
and a pair of muscled arms. Nights I dreamed

that the great blue heron folded her wings and entered
the water like a stone, like the woman who jumped

from the bridge a mile upriver — her blue dress surfacing
the same shade as our mother's, the river mending the hole

they made, water glinting like the surface of a coin,
air shimmering with dragonflies and Daddy's thin blue smoke.

4

ON THE GREAT PLAINS' EASTERN EDGE

People here don't dream of falling, but the opposite
of falling — of drying up and being blown

across the far-flung horizon during months of drought
when topsoil embeds itself in every surface —

sheets hung on the line to dry, shut eyelids,
hair up in a braid, firmly clamped lips —

when even good roots can't hold and there's no water
left in the well to wash it all clean. Every year — *pause just here*

Lopping

when the twisters come there's a new story
about your grandmother's neighbor pulled from sleep

and shaken like a tablecloth before being dropped
in the family plot to rest beside her husband,

fish string

dead these twenty years, or the minister and his wife plucked
from the closet where they huddled clutching the Bible

and each other and set down without a scratch
in the yard, not even a ripped page to show for it.

When the rains do come, by God's own grace
and after a dozen farmers are dead from self-inflicted

important of Harvest

gunshot wounds or a noose swung over the hayloft's beam,
those who remain dream of the swelling up, the washing

away and slow drowning — a different kind of falling.
Our bloated bodies come to rest in the muck

5

of gray-green lakes. The silt makes room,
shifts in the gloom and the bluegills come, curious,

the pike, resilient, to nibble at cotton fibers,
spitting out buttons and clasps to get at the heavy, rotting flesh.

lots of these poems.

LOVER, SAY PRAIRIE

Say *prairie* and mean an underground sea
watering the roots of tall grasses that sway
like the thin bodies of girls dressed in sackcloth.
Mean the sharp angles of sodbusting plows
that mirror the men who guide them, whittled down
by work, weather, and wind, men down to sinew
and sweat, down to a stunning silence.

the best? the effects of very good.

Say *prairie* and mean the song of the canary,
caged to accompany the lone woman
in her house made of dirt and sod, the one
window, a warped portal looking out on the flat
horizon, miles and miles until the sky weds the land,
a hazy, indistinct joining, the way their two bodies
meet under a quilt in the insect-loud night.

the canary and woman

7

FENCE LINE TO HILL RISE

Across this prairie, the Laurentide Ice Sheet
left behind boulders the size of combines
and grain trucks, the kind of rock
that refuses to be dug up, that demands
to be given into and gone around.

Today, echoes of the receding ice
sound in the plow blade's long rasp,
unzipping the spring soil, opening
a furrow from fence line to hill rise.
Every farmer knows the feel, the taste
of good dirt — the glacial drift that sifted
into the scarred crust and evened us out,
made these acres fertile and sacred,
gave birth to prairie grass
and rivers fanned like fingers.

Smaller stones rise up each year,
heaved to the surface by frost
to clank against the disk blades,
forcing us to reclaim the fields.
The earth gives birth to what it wants,
fodder for cairns at the fence corners.

BORN WITHOUT

Born to the voice-swallowing plains,
to winds that scour and erase the ancestral slate,
to the prairie empty of graves that bear
my family names, I do my own divining.
The voices of my Scandinavian dead
elude me on this shelterless land.

In another version of this lifetime
the village crones would teach me
to read the cards or bones or leaves.
I only know what my mother knows,
how to foretell the threat of building storms,
when to call in the herd, when to abandon
them to the orange-green tornado birthing sky.

9

INHERITANCE

Our fathers walk with wrecked knees, bowed
by the heave and pitch of their fathers'
heirloom
and grandfathers' patched together farms,
by years of bad shocks on the Massey Ferguson.

They stand in dry September's stubble fields and read
next spring's drainage by the way their heels settle —

bootprints that fill up with grit the minute
they step away. These men learn to swallow

the gravel of defeat and grind their teeth to nubs.
Even a good year keeps them silent,

their eyes squinting hard across a horizon
that stretches and arcs too far for one man to hold.

they're trying to do we then up
men come do.

DUTY

It's the father's duty to comfort the sick child,
her ear a small red dish, warm to his touch.
He presses it against his flannel/chest —
the rhythm of his rocking, his distant heartbeat,
the soft words he repeats above her head,
her only entrance to sleep.

The child grows out of his reach.
She dodges his confessions, and her ear
becomes a funnel, letting the morsels
of his slick speech loop through. The ear
no longer aches, no longer leans
toward any other body.

11

DUTY, REVISITED

It's the daughter's duty to save the father.
Once she's grown and called to the bedside, — his old —
she must answer, must return to a man   he helped her when she
flailing and lost, to admit her part,   was young.
the female Prospero in her who raised
the tempest brewing in his mind.
she did leave —   on he own accord.
(Knowing the thousand-mile distance
is of her own making, she travels
with words beading on her lips,
incantations that surface from a book
she swallowed years ago. Her voice
is small, and she is afraid it will not carry,
will not be heavy enough to survive
the depression's gale force winds.

fighting a grave
disease

Duty to leave and
to return

12

FACING HOME

Every farmer is in the field, plow blades
tearing at the dormant earth, and now I know
my father's depression is as black
as these northeast Iowa fields, muddied
by the thunderstorms that roll over the plains
in waves, bogging everything down for days.
I arrive to find he moves like he's coated in sludge,
heaviness cleaving to his willow-thin body
and pulling down. I walk the fence-rows,
facing home on the edge of a cold front,
herding the wind I believe will be enough
to whip the weight away from his frame,
restoring whatever it was he once believed in.

The door rattles with my entrance, the house
swallowing sound, returning to silence.
I am here for a week to watch his erosion
through the time-lapse photography of visits
spaced months apart, wondering what state
I'll find him in when the corn stalks tower
above the farmers, the ears thick with kernels
and topped with the banners of slick silks.
For now, we tamp the fear down with the advice
of doctors and trips to the pharmacy,
passing tractors with neon orange triangles
that warn us to move slowly around machinery
that is burdened and bulging with seed.

13

ROOFING THE BARN

The roof, stripped down to plywood sheets,
shone like the mahogany coat of the gelding
knee-deep in pasture, both swaybacked with age.
Spreading the tarpaper in great swathes,
we tasted sawdust and oil, anchoring it
with the repeated firing of the staple gun.
Next day the shingles slid in the morning cool,
rasped against themselves, the roof, our gloves,
and resisted the short, blunt nails.
By noon they stuck, silent in piles.
Nothing sounded on the roof's steep slope
but the thud of hammers and shuffling boots
trying to keep a grip. My father worked the edges
and around the vents, whittling curves and slants
and making sure the notches matched.
I climbed the peak and straddled the ridge,
looking out across the acres of corn.
The order of the fields, the way the corners met,
was a kind of faith, as reassuring as the line of shingles,
as a green that stayed straight all the way to the horizon.

the land and the farm is all of
like for so many farmers.

LABOR DAY ON THE BREMER BLACKTOP

My grandparents' Buick is wide,
      rides smooth
on this newly minted asphalt as we visit
half-forgotten cemeteries
near Nashua,
   Chickasaw,
     and Charles City,
grass grown up in the ruts of tree-lined drives.

Alongside the car, barn swallows
      swoop and skim ditches
full of bursting cattails and milkweed pods,
everything gone to seed at last,
even the field on my grandfather's farm —

three decades now out of our hands,
     out of the almanac in our blood.

The alfalfa stalks brush
     the broad chest
of an Appaloosa mare. Along her flank,
my grandfather calls up the ghosts of his Clydesdale team:
    Dot, Beauty, Byrd, and Spot.

Everything capable grazes beneath a fleet of clouds.

In the field's southwest corner
a granite boulder
    shoulders the horizon
like a sack of feed, sun catching mica flints
in the rock's grain,
    dazzling as any city skyline at dusk.

THE BRIDGE AT BURLINGTON

Driving through the limbo of a light rain
in the black belly of this river basin,

I count the miles until the crossing over,
the leap from bank to bank when nothing

but a faith in physics holds us all up
while the muddy sludge and the barges

whisper below. Waiting ten miles ahead,
the bridge at Burlington is all rivets,

all intercostal cement and steel, wrenching close
the ribs of Iowa and Illinois, and I am westbound,

returning in rain and the caesura of a soft night,
the fertile dirt drunk from a good soaking and open

to the seed. The ridges along the riverbank,
darker than the night, fold me in and I am planted

deeper into the terrain with every mile.
These are the roads my grandfather drives,

his course as gradual and sluggish as the river,
his breathing labored. There's nothing to be done.

SIXTY MILES TO PECULIAR

A dozen creeks left to cross —
      Pole Cat, Sugar Fork, Thief Hollow —
the car dipping slightly, a descent
                    into each watershed,

as it thunders across the riggings of old stone bridges,
past concrete edges
that never, no matter how much the contractors
      measure and weigh,
              align.

This land, like the flanks of the black Angus,
heaves on spring's wet abundance,
          deflates in summer's drought,
turns its haunches into the stubborn wind,
opening and closing its wet, glazed eyes.

There are some questions we never find the answers to.

Another creek,
        another curve and a rise buoying
the belly of the car and I could sail out over the plains —

a new prairie schooner,
a new species of hawk

soaring above the gold dust,
      the red chili pepper earth.

MIDNIGHT CROSSING OKLAHOMA

Only the road
        and the artificial horizon of headlights
fluctuate in the studied stillness.

This dark traveling, cast out and alien,
      alters time and space,
pushes me past the place where stars begin,
where the radio picks up voices, and in the largest
                pockets of absence,
picks up the echo of voices.

Static seeps into a preacher's rusted voice
and lets a country song slide over its back
so that God and Lefty Frizzell —
               duke it out between the overpasses.

The sky out west of Tulsa spits stars.
     They break up into microscopic light
and crowd the hood of my truck
             like hieroglyphics.

GREEN MOUNTAIN FALLS

— Elevation 6410 Feet

Day breaks
        knife-like and sudden
across the spine of this pine-covered mountain.

Walking downtown in the still shadowed
streets, it's the light
        glowing through the frosted glass
of a coffee shop's front window
that reminds me of the prairie dawn
        softened by fields of beans and wheat
                into birthlight,
the gradual opening at the end of night's long closure,
the gentle hand lifting the black veil.

This is the way I choose to enter the world.   *alone*

Back home on the family farm
when summer edges
        toward fall,
    the sun comes up through fog
and the hayfield breathes out a jeweled breath.

My last day there I stand on a slight rise
and cast my finely-woven net over
those rough acres,
        pulling in the grasshopper's
emerald teeth, the shed scales of the luna moth's
trembled wing, the corn tassel's pollen,
and all the lace-knit webs
        cradling those still-beating hearts.

the life in the prairie

NOTES FROM THE CABIN
ON SHILOH MOUNTAIN

The wind-tipped terracotta pot
spills last year's leached dirt
and a tangle of vines.

No one remembers to latch
the gate completely. It complains
of the wind while worshipping it.

The pileated woodpecker taunts
me with its drumming. It flies
along the tree-line, trim as a torpedo.

(A portable propane tank and a wrench
left on the porch signify something
human that I'm not ready to admit.)

At eventide the red wasp wants
this last patch of sun. We tolerate
each other's buzz and hum.

both need to tolerate – equality

On the horizon, the turkey vultures
ride the day's last thermals
with more grace than I can muster.

(We are all just packing
our own sack of bones.)
The weight is in the marrow.

respect for animals' agendas.

IN HER MOTHER'S COUNTRY

In her mother's country, she's a green seed
humming — sub-acoustic — the husk

about to break open, revealing the first root.
She stirs to the song the women sing when they dig

the shallow holes and toss in the unblinking eyes
of potatoes saved back for planting, tamping

the mounds of black dirt with their feet.
In that far north country, land of aurora borealis

and the remnants of glaciers from another age,
where her mother was born in the bloomtime

and named for the sound of petals unfolding,
she will arrive early with her two eyes open,

one fist clenched, the other hand a flat plain,
and they will struggle to find her proper name.

a fitting end

struggle

fu chonging human face/ person.

MOMENTARY CONSTELLATIONS:
12 SELF-PORTRAITS

JANUARY

Garnet month of my birth,
this winter my thirty-first,
my bed of snow. All month, desire
throbs like the heat of banked embers —
light source in the dark nights,
mirror to the flame of the cardinal's crest —
crushed silk among the birch branches.
When the bird sings, I swallow the notes like seeds,
like a miracle prayed for and delivered.
I'm cooped up and burning.
I open my mouth to echoes.

FEBRUARY

The coffee shop is lit by a staggering sun.
Golden stalks of light elongate and collapse
across my lap. Two bright oranges, sectioned
on a dish, capture the light, revealing my real name.
It is the sound of the train whistle muted by snow,
phonetics I write on a scrap of napkin.
Walking home along the tracks, I uncover the bones
of an unknown animal — the ribs ten inches long
from tip to weathered tip. Remnants of skin
and muscle wave like flags. All day I breathe carefully.
Nothing has touched me in weeks. My boundaries grow
solid and delicate as glass bending light.

MARCH

And this is the way she makes the world
feather by waxed feather
fixed to the balsa bone of a frame
of a wing she found buried in snow
last December. She waits
until all the porch lights are off
for the night, then draws her bundles out
from behind piles of rags, dusty quarts of oil,
and albums gathering grit in their grooves,
distorting voices that bounce and rattle —
a language that breaks like sweetness
across her tongue. In the dark,
she works by touch and by the smell
of extinguished acetylene torches,
fresh twine, and the wood glue's bitter root.
Deep in the throat of the night, she falters and falls
asleep, head resting among the cast off
debris on the work bench, one hand
still reaching to stroke this new thing
that unfurls in the dank hours
when she dreams into existence the key,
cool as porcelain, bitter as copper-plating,
tucked under her tongue.

[handwritten annotation: but isn't actually real]

APRIL

Dear S —

All week the small bushes pushed
out their new leaves, splashes
of bright yellow-green crowding
the low hills, breaking apart winter's
cold patina. News of M —' s disease
last Christmas settled on my heart
like snow, the kind that stays.
This thaw is hard-pressed to clear
the ice floes in my veins.

Today, I watch from my window
as buds appear on the willows
lining the creek. I'm enclosing
one new growth, still warm, almost furry.
I lick it like a stamp, paste it to the page
still green, wondering how it will reach you.

MAY

What I know is that fear begins
in the blindness of love or lust.
When I was two I longed to live in water,
threw my body three times into the pool
and let it sink, my mouth open like a goldfish
and breathing in. They hauled me out,
each time slapping the water from my lungs
the way my grandmother beat dirt from a rug.
My legs grew rooted in the safety
of solid ground, and I abandoned
the language of fish for the sound
of things that could be drowned.

JUNE

after Lucie Brock-Broido

Am aerial. Am light catcher and reflector —
flickering goldfinch wing, patch of blood
on the blackbird's shoulder. Am wind lover.

Am six river pebbles sucked dry,
stories of fish, limestone, and lakeweed.
Am the skeletal remains spit into the palm.

Am eighteen hours of sun grafted to the horizon.
Am plow guide. Am farmer and furrow,
fresh green spear slicing through topsoil and fertilizer.

Am lilac blooms. Am clinging
and clung to — the bee's sweaty palm
pressed on skin, collecting.

Am the two days' traveling, body of driveshaft
and wheel. Am metamorphosis from plains to mountain.
Am tinder thick and drought-stricken.

Am the continuously struck match.
Am fire, wind-licked and thrown, crown to crown.
Am driven and unstoppable.

JULY

Near the creek all month, a stench seeps
and hovers, something half-buried, rotten,
a cloaked and rampant green. At night,
when I pause to watch the fireflies marking
momentary constellations, I don't stand long.
The air is heavy with the desire to claw beneath
the surfaces of things — the creek bank so thick
with growth, no one claims the land.
All month, I am alone in my bed, and the fan
has lost the strength to push the air.
Heat lightning. Then none. Longing
digs in this way — like rain, like the train
you wait for derailed miles up the track.

AUGUST

This then is the mirror she faces daily:
full-length with beveled edge,
                                waiting.
In the lamplight, she charts the contours
of her body, traces the rivers of her veins
and the lined skin's uneven terrain,
a necessary navigation.
                         Possession
being nine-tenths of the law,
she patrols the borders of her territory
under the mirror's watchful eye,
noting microscopic changes with precision,
believing this map will be her ticket
to love or salvation,
                      whatever's coming next.
The X-marks-the-spot is her secret weapon,
the thing that she withholds when she pens
each day's new data on the vellum — slick
and opal-colored, darker where her hands
gather the ungainly edges in and fold them over
and over the same creases the mirror reflects.

lonely - needs to look Sorry

[strikethrough: Hea]

needs more desirable

feature.

SEPTEMBER

The girl on the Shetland pony tosses
her head, shaking hay and bits of chaff
out of her matted hair while the pony strains
against the bridle, wanting to get the bit
in its teeth and lower its head
to what remains on the mown field.
The pony has been known to founder,
to gorge itself on summer's last lush
until its stomach bloats and its legs grow thick
as silos standing staunch against the sky.
The girl's hands on the reins hold back
that need, the fringe on her jacket
mingling with the pony's mane.

OCTOBER

Month I became the silent child,
the mortar of the brick wall crumbling,
everything come loose as a baby tooth.

Air rushed in, whistled on the way out,
my body as dry as an Egyptian tomb.
Voices tumbled in, forced open
the shut ear, made me the depository,
this library of spurn and scorn.

Month I became the thorn,
venom, muscle and the flat hand,
became a word that pulsed
and writhed and was unsayable.

NOVEMBER

Walking home in the first hard freeze
with ice building in layers on the slick surfaces
of roads and bridges, my breath plumes
before me and I cough on the brittle air.
I tread on the safer grass-lined ditch,
the creek bank's thick mud, stiff like setting plaster.
The sun fades behind the trees, and I am insular,
wrapped in a dim, sky-heavy day and counting
the weeks until spring unlocks winter's leaden door.

When the forecast calls for the worst,
I let the tap in the stainless steel sink
run all night and I dream of songbirds,
warblers and orioles, their pipe-cleaner legs
trapped on iced-over branches, too exhausted
to do anything but sing. Their orange
and yellow feathers drop to the snow —
false flames I gather in my bare hands
and bring to my mouth in hunger.
I wake to the sound of the water heater kicking in,
to the metallic bite of birch bark and rust in my throat.

DECEMBER

Too long alone again and words clutter,
hover behind my clenched teeth, my mouth
no longer sure what slight adjustments equal speech.

My tongue is the petal of a tulip touched by frost.
My throat, in the next year, will belong to the hawk
or the fat, black garden snake lying dormant
now in the crawlspace beneath the house.

Winter is made of this muteness and these windows
and the long view of white fields through icy glass
where nothing moves and nothing raises its voice.

LISTENING IN THE DARK

THE EMPTY SET, RECURRING

No members, no elements to speak of.
                                        With nothing
left to say, she resides in the white asylum of solitude.

A bird on the branch refusing to sing.

She throws pebbles into onion grass,
wanting to scare, with a ripple on the still surface,

                                        any living thing
into movement. She is pond-flat, trapped
in central standard time —
                            the mundane flood of sun,
the moon slung low over fields,
the eyes' long-distance lope to the horizon.

Her fever comes each midnight, rises flush against the skin,
and she does not fight it,
                            believing the sweat and the sweet
residual musk will draw the ache away like lips
suctioned against the snakebite,
                            a cleansing ritual of last resort.
Lacking the punctured wound,
she settles for the heat of her heart as it pumps —
                    four chambers large enough to echo back
all the sounds she thinks she silenced.

not gone – just repressed

SHE KNOWS

What is it like to be a woman
listening in the dark?
                    — *Anne Carson*

To be a woman listening in the dark
is not about the neon murmur of night,

not about falling asleep with her ear
still scanning the flat horizon.

A woman listening in the dark is done
waiting for the encrypted return signal.

The thin silver cord holding closed
her night-colored robe is the way

she lashes herself to the world,
her chair the cement block weighing

her body down in the black current.
At her window she tracks falling stars,

her body beneath her clothes emitting
a color of light beyond any spectrum.

held done by herself
and surrondings

40

UNMOORED ABSENCE

The sky cloudy for nights on end,
the polestar swallowed. Adrift

in the trackless desert. Here is the sextant,
useless in my hand. Here, the wick-spark

of match after match struck. The gasp
into flame. The dowsing wind.

The solid surface of the world slips,
curls up to envelop the clouds that clutch

at the edge of the sky. This is the result
of the hard choice to move through the world

alone, to have given up on the universe,
while the slow expansion of galaxies

grinds closer to the moment gravity
lets loose of us all.

INCARNATIONS

My previous bodies:
a wooden boat,
a tangle of vines inching up the ruins,
a misnamed saint poisoned and preserved.

There is never an escape, a rest,
from the audience and its eye.
O, Reader, you leer and peer
and pry, but I have helped you
loosen the fence board. Tho' I am shy.

My current bodies:
an impatient seed,
a yellow-headed blackbird blown off course,
an orphan rescued and returned to her ordinary name.

I go about without a wedding garment.
You, my confidant, my confider,
lie down with me amid the barley
and the wheat, dandelion chains
coiling our ankles and our feet.

this seems out
of place in the
part of the
book

My future bodies:
a swayed pine,
a perfume brewed from teak and spice,
a woman silked and webbed, crystallized.

AND THIS TOO WILL BE A DIFFICULT BEARING

My personal lifeguard turns
the taut, tan skin of his cheek
away from the glare of midday sun
on sea, away from the empty space
I create as I struggle in the salt-bitten waves.

I try to recall the shape of *floatation*,
the way the physicist diagrammed
a body bobbing on the ocean,
the simple way lungs and muscles
lulled to relaxation equaled buoyancy.

The equation fails, fills with sand, and sinks,
light fracturing as I am taken under.

RECKONING THE FRAGMENTS

Days after my lover abandoned me,
a controlled burn in the state forest
flooded the town with smoke.
The sun filtered to muted gold
so precious I tried to cup it
in my ice-laced hands.

This is the painful epilogue.

All night I heat the tongs,
patient as a blacksmith,
my body strapped to the bed,
one arm, still free to plunge
in, to cauterize the bleeding heart.
  grewsome
These are the first blue hours of spring.

This is the painstaking thaw,
the turning of the lathe and axis
as the world spins at equinox.
My closest friend offers *equilibrium*
as a word my heart could use
as a bandage or a cast.
I misspell it every time,
tossing these scraps of paper
in the tinderbox amidst the kindling
that waits for the next spark.

love thrown to the fire.

LONGING AT 17,000 FEET

On a clear day, she drives to the airport,
puts the car in long-term parking, and tries to forget.
This happens two days after she's gotten drunk
and curled herself into the arms of a strange man,

lips and limbs colliding for hours. In a window seat,
in the last instant that the wheels remain in contact
with the ground, she remembers one kiss —
his lips left hers and she saw that the sky
had turned blue without her permission.

She leaves the shade up, watches the plane's shadow
cross the unnamable river beneath her, and thinks
that's the way, cool as water. Some rivers have muscles
that can only be seen from the sky.

ANOTHER LOVE POEM ABOUT LEAVING

The shape of you leaving
was the shape of the brown bear
wheeling on his hind legs,
snout turned into the wind,
catching the scent of salmon
torn open by the sharp rocks
in the shallow river.

The sun struck golden haunches
and ricocheted into shadows
as you shouldered through the brush,
breaking a fresh trail. And then,
the dark closing, the aftermath,
the tremble going out of the branches,
this new stillness the only evidence
of the shape of you leaving.   *arde the Geck up*

That was the moment I prayed
to be turned to stone, to dust,
to water, to anything born
without a heart, senseless and numb.
I waited weeks without an answer,
until the first piercing pain ebbed
to an ache, until I finally turned
and took my unchangeable body,
my misshapen heart, home.

HELIOPAUSE

The pedestal I raised you to was made
of fiberglass and tissue paper flames.
I hoisted you up with my favorite crane

and pulled the lever for your voice —
for the first part
crushed gravel sound of your lips,
divinity dispersed in wisps, a sound
that succored and soothed me.

I pedaled in pollen and pearls for you

and was sentenced to the blue rooms
of purgatory, where I studied
my astrophysical book of hours

until this revelation came unfastened:

after the solar wind retracts and the shroud
of this green world returns to ice, even you
will shrink to the size of a regular god.

*like the
Rapture*

FEBRUARY SOUTH WINDS

These days, when my heart contracts
to that small space,

        less than a pebble,

dense with loss, I long for the secret diary,

        for the drop

            of pollen sucked from clover,

for smoother sounds than this rough lexicon
of arctic air and snow

        hardening in jagged piles.

I turn my face to the bluer sky,
make tree-sounds,

        creek-ice breaking-up sounds,

and look to the breeze for its quickening release.

WAYS TO STAY WARM IN WINTER

Split the flesh of a blood orange.
Buy a pair of spine-cheek anemone fish

and set their bowl on the cold, slate hearth.
Store barrels of kerosene behind the molting couch.

Become your own spark and the delay
on the delicate fuse that only you can disarm.

Insulate the faulty wiring of your faultless heart.
Accept the weight, the heft of snow.

MARCH AFTERNOON

Emergency flare of a sun,
                                an empty sky.

Wind gusts ruffle the remains of last year's tall grasses —

               the stand of ornamental pampas
                         and the pond rushes gone brown and dry.

I am talking to the hawk and the horizon when I say:

                              Stun me.

Pull me from this winter coma.
Cleave me open
               like sod split by the plow.
                                   Lay me bare.

The red wasps hang in the air,
                              dangerous question marks.
          The sun slides toward the tree line,

collides with a forming cloud —
                         a muscular light blooms.

ASLEEP IN MATING SEASON

Mid-spring, and a late freeze this far south
shrouds the city in hoarfrost. The wind,
careening around corners, calls me out of my name.
I stumble on every doorsill, my mouth
roundly opened, the hint of a response
that bleeds off like the last breath
of oxygen in the tank escaping.
All night I dream of three children pulled
up from the mud-sponged river bank,
water cascading brown down the slope
of their onion-white skin. They bleed
from their navels and are not the ones
I gave birth to, not my darlings of dense hair
and finely sculpted toes. Those I left cradled
on the back of a horse that moved seamlessly
beneath us, canter smooth as flight.

ETUDE

After my daughter learned to dance, I called
her *Stepping Water*. She walked with that much grace.
Some days I watched her test the law of gravity —
the wind her patient lover. With a threat
like that, I only did what any mother
would do. I weighted her with gems and coins
sewn in the hems of her long scarves and skirts.
Earthbound, my wounded kite, she would not be consoled.
When I stroked her hair, warm from gathering
the sunlight falling thick as rain through her window,
she no longer pressed her head into my palm —
once her sign of sure forgiveness. Now she pulls away.
I watch her stretch her liquid limbs.
I check the seams of silk for evidence of wear,
numbering my days in the time it takes
a thread to fray. In my nightmares, she gifts
the hills with her bounty-weight as she twirls
and twirls, until all that's left is silk.

PSALM FOR THE COLOR RED

What do you do with the boy who never learns
about the crawlspace under the stairs
just the size of his body, who never accepts
that the shadows in his bedroom aren't alive,
who puts his hand on the burner
because the explosion of pain is the color red,
like her hair that he wraps in his sweaty fist,
like the shoes she gave him with secret wings.
In church they sing about flying away,
and the feathers begin to move. He starts to dance,
just a little, in the boy-sized space between the pews.
How do you make still what won't be still?
A hand, heavy as the hymnal, comes down on his shoulder,
attempting to douse the embers hissing in his hair,
the flames leaping from his tapping, tapping feet.

if we are happy / if is suppressed

LIGHT

I watch my second son sideways.
He's made of too much light to risk
direct exposure. My private sand dollar,
fragile treasure, he is fond of saying things like,
The difference between clear skies and clouds
is the difference between being alone and being lonely.
When he speaks, his mouth emits a yellow glow
and if he moves, he flings transparent strands
less sticky than a spider's thread but just as strong.
I keep him wrapped in cotton,
dark, organic colors gathered from deep places —
the horizon several hours past midnight, the trench
on the sea floor, the walls of the abandoned mine.
This depth makes him safe enough to hold.
It's the edges of things that attract him most.
In winter when he can stand to leave the house,
he balances where the roof ends and the sky begins.

not an adulterous child

flat word is
every where

ANOTHER MEMORY FRAGMENT

The year I was seven, my mother
came home from the hospital
with stitches and a black box
in which she guarded a moon.
She carried it wearing gloves,
opening it when she wanted
her three excitable girls to be still.
That was the summer we suffered
from the rain. A continual dowsing
kept us cooped up and molding.

The night we finally banded together,
snuck along the damp baseboards,
and slipped past her bed to take
the box, I swear the light leaked out
through the seams and touched us
like the breath of a god too intimate
to bear. Our skin glowed and burned,
and we became, in that moment,
unmistakably like her, transformed,
like her, incurably tame.

NIGHT TRAIN

There are nights the train rages
through the curve of the tracks
outside her room and she's shaken
by the urge to force its leap
from the rails ground smooth by sparks.

The headlight strobes
through tree trunks and brush,
pushing forward what is hunted
across the snow-dusted plains.
In her room, she presses her cheek
to the icy window, anticipating
a violence of shattered glass.

What she wants is never to fade,
to live everything in the space
where the sound grows larger
than the dark absence of the moon.

RECITATION DURING THE STORM

Let the thunder clamor above and continue
after lightning has licked the heavy air.

This is not a haunting. I mean to be awake
and wide-eyed — to be both owl and field mouse
caught in strobes of light.

The clock pushes past midnight, then one,
then two, and I am counting backwards
into what is left as the bruises fade.

One man told me love was a transitive verb,
worrying me like a rosary bead to prove it.
Another man stood me in the middle of Nebraska
to prove the Permian seas once stretched
from Pittsburgh to Denver, home to creatures
we read about with our stone-caressing fingers
but could never know. The last man was a thief,
his voice a prayer to a god so exotic I bloodied
my knees falling down before them both.

This is a recounting. I mean to be accurate
and true — to be both diary and document
held open and up to the light.

Let the storm pass, dawn taming the landscape
outside my room, leaves and branches loosening
back into the shapes of trees.

THE BRIGHTENING HOUR

Midmorning, when the sky gives way from cloud
to sun and hawks perch in the top branches

of trees still blackened by last night's rain,
I become all breath, too alive for this world.

what does / that mean

This is the radiant hour of a land unleashed.
All I can do is stare as the blue jays feed

in the fence-row under the shelter of neglected
brush, small tufts of porcelain blue revealed,

a frenzy of feather and seed and beak,
of hunger and need and the given feast.

NIGHTS WHEN IT RAINS

after reading John Dufresne

While you sleep, I prop the window open,
listening to the rain drum the surface
of the lake, the fat magnolia leaves,
the stretched canvas of the hammock.
I think about the way water infiltrates
all the fractured places, circulates
through stone, the way it seeps and filters,
the way it makes room for what enters —
body or boat or lure — and then closes
neatly behind what leaves. The human body
is more water, I know, than muscle or bone,
and my heart beats the rhythm of rain,
my fingers wandering just above your skin,
desperate as the fog to engulf you. *how brutal*

But she doesn't

CROSSING THE ARKANSAS

A red buoy marks the channel,
and catfish clutter the bottom,
slow mud movers dredging
their own furrows in the dark —
sunrise to them a mere lightening
of the gloom. You and I stop
here on the Broadway Bridge,
homeless men ranging like wolves
along the shore beneath us.
Their arms hang bare from torn-off
sleeves. To the left a barge
eases its bulk downriver, laden
with grain and severing the fog
like a hand through a spiderweb.
When I try to speak to you
about the nature of endurance,
you squint sideways into the sun
and flip the visor down, casting
everything above your lips into shadow.

She lives in Arkansas

SUNDAYS, DRIVING AWAY FROM YOU

Night comes down in slow increments
      on these Arkansas back roads,
            trees gathering dusk in the leaves
like flocks of birds —
              daily migrations of light.

Melancholy haunts the fluid horizon.

      Just past the reach of the headlights' glow
the silhouette of a horse
        grazes on the ridge, it's body a bruise
              darker than the night.

All week we will move
            through the business of days
      separated by these piney bayous,
         miles of seeping rivers and the interrupted
transmission of cellular phones —
              your voice
      in my ear, in the husky hour of sleep
         will be an earnest, broken heat.

FROM THE OUTPOST

The wind is in the pampas-grass today,
a sound like flames rushing through tinder.

From the doorway, I've called to you three times,
your name a trumpet of its own and silver
on my scuttled tongue. The frogs make answer,
something half-cricket, half-bird and newly emerged
from the mud. Their song lures me into thaw.

For now, I've left a week's worth of laundry
on the line while I doze in the first sharp sun
since the days turned round the equinox
and slowly began to lengthen. Listen!
The earth gives back the ice by seeping.

Your last note said, "Still no hummingbirds"
and included a sketch of the ruby throat
and spindly beak. I tucked it behind the nest
we found last fall, woven with lichen
and spider silk. When you see them hover
at the lip of the bee balm and jewelweed,
pack your bags. Send word to me.

this is a freedom song

where is the tension

POSTSCRIPT

TO MY DOCENT WHO HAS TAKEN HIS LEAVE

My elucidator. My excavator.
What do you make of this, my latest document?

The paper is imported — culled & contraband.
With my tongue I paid to have the edges frayed.

I confess, the crows here are raucous,
the caw, the caw, persistent as the rain.
They interfere.

You will say I grip the pen too hard.
I do. I dip the tip in oil.
It slides. It slinks.
My ravisher! My rescuer!
These letters sink.

The mornings here are an agony
of ice, of ice, sharp as the butcher's blade.
It punctuates the air.

What leaves were left have fallen — brown & brittle.
The wind takes hold and I refuse the rake.

You will say I turn the heat too high.
I do. I wrap myself in wool.
I thaw. I ache.
My inoculist. My interloper.
I shall let this missive bake.

NOTES

"1976"
Owes its beginnings to Charles Wright's "1975."

"Black Dirt Girls"
Emmylou Harris' song "Red Dirt Girl" influenced the title
of this poem.

"Incarnations"
Grew in response to Cyril Connolly's *The Unquiet Grave*.

"June"
Lucie Brock-Broido's poem "Am Moor" shaped the structure
of this poem.

"Midnight Crossing Oklahoma" and "Sixty Miles to Peculiar"
Arose after reading Charles Wright's *Zone Journals*.

"Nights When It Rains"
John Dufresne's story "The Way That Water Enters Stone" sparked
this poem.

"On the Great Plains' Eastern Edge"
Opening lines inspired by a passage in William Least Heat-Moon's
Prairy Erth.

"Roofing the Barn"
My reply to Seamus Heaney's "Thatcher."

"She Knows"
Epigraph comes from Anne Carson's *Autobiography of Red*.

ABOUT THE AUTHOR

Sandy Longhorn was born in Waterloo, Iowa in 1971 and received her BA in English from the College of St. Benedict (MN) in 1993. In 2003 she received an MFA from the University of Arkansas at Fayetteville. Currently, she teaches at Pulaski Technical College and lives in Little Rock, Arkansas.

THE ANHINGA PRIZE FOR POETRY

Blood Almanac
Sandy Longhorn, 2005

Ornithologies
Joshua Poteat, 2004

Orchidelirium
Deborah Landau, 2003

Inventory at the All-night Drugstore
Erika Meitner, 2002

Tackle Box
Patti White, 2001

Singular Bodies
Ruth L. Schwartz, 2000

Notations on the Visible World
Kathleen Wakefield, 1999

Practicing for Heaven
Julia B. Levine, 1998

Conversations During Sleep
Michele Wolf, 1997

Man Under a Pear Tree
Keith Ratzlaff, 1996

Easter Vigil
Ann Neelon, 1995

*Mass for the Grace
of a Happy Death*
Frank X. Gaspar, 1994

The Physicist at the Mall
Janet Holmes, 1993

Hat Dancer Blue
Earl S. Braggs, 1992

Hands*
Jean Monahan, 1991

The Long Drive Home*
Nick Bozanic, 1989

Enough Light to See
Julianne Seeman, 1988

Conversing with the Light*
Will Wells, 1987

The Whistle Maker*
Robert Levy, 1986

Perennials*
Judith Kitchen, 1985

The Hawk in the Backyard
Sherry Rind, 1984

Sorting Metaphors
Ricardo Pau-Llosa, 1983

*Out of print